Hope for the Hidden

Empowering the young carer

Maria Machí

Illustrations by Irina Akimkina
Cover design by Mab Rose – mabrose.com

This book is published by
Grosvenor House Publishing Ltd
Link House
140 The Broadway, Tolworth, Surrey, KT6 7HT.
www.grosvenorhousepublishing.co.uk

A CIP record for this book
is available from the British Library

ISBN 978-1-80381-766-8
eBook ISBN 978-1-80381-767-5

Dedication

This book is lovingly dedicated to my husband, Marcin. His unwavering belief in me and his constant support have been the pillars of strength throughout this journey. Marcin, your encouragement and love have made all the difference, and this achievement is as much yours as it is mine.

I also dedicate this work to the young carers who have been both my inspiration and my teachers. Their resilience, compassion, and wisdom have shaped the pages of this book. To these heroes, thank you for allowing me to learn from your experiences.

Contents

Disclaimer

In this book Olivia's story is fictitious. Names, characters, businesses, places, events, locations and incidents are either the product of the author's imagination or used in a fictitious manner. Any resemblance to actual persons, living or dead, or actual events is purely coincidental.

The information presented in this book is intended for informational purposes only and is not comprehensive. It is not designed to replace professional consultation, diagnosis or medical treatment. Always seek the advice of a mental health professional or other qualified health practitioners with any questions you may have regarding a medical condition or mental health concerns.

The author is not responsible for any specific health needs that may require medical supervision and is not liable for any damages or negative consequences from any treatment, action, application to any person reading or following the information in this book. References are provided for informational purposes only and do not constitute endorsement of any websites or other sources.

If you suspect someone is facing a mental health emergency or another medical urgency, it is imperative to seek immediate medical assistance. Do not neglect professional advice or delay seeking it because of something you have read in this book.

Preface

Drawing on a rich foundation in psychology and play therapy, I have dedicated my career to the complex area of young carers. My journey began at the University of Valencia, where I earned my degree in Psychology from 2003 to 2009. Seeking further specialisation, I moved to the UK to delve into the world of play therapy at the University of South Wales. It was during this time that I first encountered the term 'young carer'. My curiosity was piqued, and I delved deeper into understanding and learning about these young individuals. By 2012, I proudly held a degree in Play Therapy from the University of South Wales.

In the early stages of my career, I had the privilege of practising as a play therapist in various schools and temporary housing services dedicated to homeless families. It was during these invaluable years that I worked directly with young carers. I began to notice a pattern: many children coming to play therapy, while referred for various reasons, were actually young carers. Their roles as caregivers were undeniably influencing their lives, an observation I found both intriguing and critical.

Later on, I joined prominent organisations and clinics throughout the UK. Notably, I worked for Place2be in Cardiff, a commendable organisation devoted to offering mental health support to children within school settings. My time there only reinforced my observations. Many of the children flagged by teachers or staff for potential behavioural issues and subsequently referred to the school's counselling department were, in fact, young carers. It became increasingly clear to me how it is paramount to understand and support these young individuals in their unique challenges.

At the renowned Tavistock and Portman clinic in London, I further sharpened my skills as a psychologist and play therapist. As I interacted with patients and researched available support and resources for them, I deepened my understanding of young caring.

Following that, I started working at Action for Children in London, marking my introduction to a dedicated young carers project. It provided me with an invaluable inside look at the operations of such a project. I was directly engaged in conducting assessments, offering counselling to young carers, aiding them in schools, managing cases through advocacy, making referrals and implementing clinical interventions, among other duties.

After my time in the UK, I relocated to Malta, where I set out to explore the support systems in place for young carers. To my astonishment, I found that not only were there no dedicated services for these young individuals, but there was also a striking lack of awareness regarding their identities and the challenges they faced daily. Recognising this gap, I felt compelled to raise awareness and initiate efforts to establish supportive frameworks for these children.

Reaching out to various organisations, I was heartened to find several eager to collaborate. Notably, SOS Malta sponsored comprehensive research into the situation of young carers on the island. As the lead researcher, I was instrumental in producing a report titled 'A Study of Young Carers in Malta' published by the NGO SOS Malta. Other institutions like St Jeanne Antide and Caritas Malta took an active interest in the study's findings, allowing me to offer counselling to young carers under their aegis.

This book is the culmination of my experience and the insights acquired throughout my career. Summarising the knowledge and advice that I've gained over the past 15 years about young carers, it is my hope that it may serve to raise awareness and help create new support systems for these children. I hope that this book might be of some help to the young carers themselves. After trying to investigate what the current situation for young carers is in other countries, and finding out that there are still many countries who lack even a term for young carers, I hope writing a short and accessible book on the topic might be a small but valid contribution to the important task of raising awareness globally.

This book is for anyone who is interested in the topic and in learning how we can help and support these heroes. This book is also for any person working in, or who has an interest in, social welfare, and even for those who have never heard of young carers. The fact that you've never encountered the term 'young carers' does not mean they don't exist. Young carers are everywhere but, unfortunately, in many cases, they still remain hidden. The book is also for young carers themselves, for them to know that they are not alone and that there are people working on finding the best ways to support them. Hopefully, the book itself provides young carers with some help and guidance.

Chapter One

Olivia's Quiet Storm: A Young Carer's World

Olivia is a sweet, kind and caring 12-year-old girl who lives in east London with her mother, Jane, and her nine-year-old brother, Benjamin. Although Olivia appears to be a very normal child, her life has not been easy so far, and from a very young age she has been struggling to cope with very difficult life challenges. Jane, her mother, was diagnosed with fibromyalgia – a chronic condition in which an individual is in constant pain, is fatigued and has trouble sleeping – at the age of 34, when Olivia was only two years old. Initially, Jane handled it quite well and managed to continue with almost a normal life with the help of Olivia's dad, Harry, and medication. However, things slowly started to get worse after she gave birth to her second child, Benjamin. After the birth, Jane's physical condition got worse, and she was not able to return to her job as a cashier at the supermarket where she had been working for the past 14 years. Soon after she stopped working, she was also diagnosed with depression and had a major depressive episode. During the episode, Jane was in a constantly depressed mood, she lost interest in almost all her normal daily activities (including spending time with and looking after her children), she was constantly tired and even little things would irritate her. When her husband insisted that she needed professional help, Jane started attending psychotherapy. She was later referred to a psychiatrist who prescribed her medicine to help her come out of her depression. After a year of rest coupled with all the help that she received, Jane started to get better. She had some recurring minor depressive episodes during the following years but managed to recover every time and resume an almost normal life.

However, four years after Jane's first major depressive episode, when Olivia was eight, Olivia's father died in a tragic car accident when returning home from work. Olivia vividly remembers the moment Jane received the news of her husband's passing, she entered into an instant state of emotional shock. Olivia felt very scared and nervously called her grandmother who quickly came to their home. The next series of events, including Harry's funeral, were extremely traumatic for the whole family.

It was recommended that the whole family attend psychotherapy to help them deal with the grief and trauma. Olivia and Benjamin initially attended these sessions because their grandmother (Jane's mother), who made every effort to help the family, would make sure they did. Jane, however, has not managed to get out of her depressive state since the accident. She continued with medication and initially she also attended counselling; however, she felt that nothing was helping her and eventually refused to continue with counselling and stopped taking her medication regularly.

Following all these unfortunate events, Olivia had to learn how to help look after her mother from a very young age. When Jane was first diagnosed with fibromyalgia, Olivia's dad and grandmother went out of their way to help her. However, soon after her dad passed away, Olivia became the main carer for Jane and Benjamin. Initially, Olivia's grandmother moved in with Jane in order to help after the tragic accident, but soon after, when Olivia was nine years old, her grandmother was diagnosed with Alzheimer's, a degenerative brain condition, and quickly became unable to provide any help. Now, Olivia's grandmother lives with Jane's older sister, Alice, and needs regular care and supervision herself. Alice has also tried to be supportive of Olivia and her family since Jane's diagnosis of depression. However, Alice and her husband work full time in Manchester, which makes it difficult for them to come and help Olivia regularly due to the two-and-a-half-hour commute. They also have three children and have been carers for Olivia's grandmother since she was diagnosed with Alzheimer's, leaving almost no space for Alice to help Olivia who looks after her mother and her little brother. Alice has tried to convince Jane to move to Manchester with Olivia and Benjamin so that she and her family could better help them, but Jane has ignored the offer and completely refuses to move.

Although Olivia had already been helping to look after her mother from a very young age, the onset of caring as a sole carer was sudden and violent. She had to simultaneously deal with the grief of losing her dad, to whom she was very attached, the severe depression of her mother, and her grandmother's Alzheimer's diagnosis with the only support being her little brother and her aunt.

Olivia doesn't receive any support from her father's side of the family. Both of her grandparents passed away a long time ago, and she now only has an uncle, Henry, who lives in Scotland.

Henry and his family have never offered help to Olivia and Benjamin. They have always blamed Jane for her struggles, particularly after her diagnosis with both conditions. Olivia recalls them frequently criticising Jane, calling her a bad wife and mother. Disliking their attitude during visits and phone calls, Olivia does not consider them a reliable support system.

On a regular day when Jane is feeling depressed, Olivia wakes up at 7am and brings her medication with a glass of water. Then, Olivia prepares breakfast, helps her brother get ready for school and takes him with her to the bus. While at school, Olivia often worries whether her mother will be ok and, often, that anxiety for her mother's well-being results in a lack of concentration. During one of Jane's depressive episodes two years ago, she tried to commit suicide. Olivia found her in a very critical state after arriving home from school. Since then, Olivia has constantly been worried that it could happen again.

When the school day is over, Olivia waits for her brother and together they take the bus back home. Once they get home, Olivia will prepare a snack for everyone and they will spend some time with their mother, if she is in the mood. There are days when Jane feels so low that she can't even find the energy to get out of bed for the whole day. Olivia makes sure to help her brother with homework and starts the laundry to make sure they both have clean school clothes for the next day. Olivia also takes care of cleaning the house and tidying up; however, their home is usually quite messy as she's the only one that really takes care of it. Once she is done with these duties, Olivia prepares dinner for everyone – she usually makes something simple like sandwiches or omelettes.

Quite often on a day like this, Olivia will have left her homework until after dinner but, by then, she is usually too tired and has almost no energy to concentrate. She feels she is not achieving as good results as she would like to at school and often hears her schoolmates talking about how many hours they have studied for their exams and how they compete to see who can get the best grades. Olivia really feels that she cannot enter into this 'competition' on an even playing field as when there is an exam she never has as much time as her peers to study.

Olivia is constantly tired. She wakes up very early and goes to bed late. She has a lot of things in her head, and she worries about her mother all the time. She feels overwhelmed and lonely very often – she doesn't have anyone around who she thinks she can talk to about what is going on at home. She trusts her aunt Alice, but she knows that she lives far away and there is not much she can do to help on a daily basis. Olivia also knows that her aunt is very overwhelmed looking after her grandmother whose condition has deteriorated recently. Olivia sometimes talks to Benjamin about what they are experiencing, but she doesn't want him to worry, especially as he is only nine years old. She doesn't want him to feel the pressure that she feels. Olivia doesn't feel comfortable talking to her two best friends at school about what is happening at home because she thinks she will be judged and they won't understand.

A while ago, Olivia heard some school children saying that her mother is 'weird', which made her very sad and made her worry even more. Olivia doesn't go out with her friends after school or on the weekends because she's always busy helping out at home. She also feels different from the other children. She knows that the other children's parents often talk to each other and organise activities and outings for their kids, but Olivia's mother is never included in these conversations, and so Olivia misses out on a lot of leisure opportunities. Jane has not had good communication with Olivia's and Benjamin's teachers at school since her condition deteriorated, and this has meant that Olivia and Benjamin have been unprepared for specific activities or events on some occasions.

Once every two or three months, on Sundays, Olivia goes out with her best friend, Amy. They love to go to the shopping mall, even if they don't buy many things. They still love to walk around the stores and dream of the dresses they would like to buy when they start work and have money. They also sometimes go to the cinema, depending on what movies are playing. Olivia really loves these days out and she would like to be able to do it more often, but every time she's out, she's constantly worrying about her mother and brother. So, many times, she just decides to skip the outing and stay home with her family. Olivia very rarely shares her worries about her mother or about anything that is going on at home. She's worried that Amy won't understand it or that she will think that her mother is crazy. She also worries sometimes about other people finding out about her mother's illness and involving social services because she's scared they could separate the family.

Olivia has been feeling very sad and depressed recently, but she feels she needs to be strong because her family needs her. Her marks at school have been getting worse over the past year, and her teachers have been constantly reminding her that she needs to put more effort in and dedicate more time to her studies. Her social life has become almost non-existent, except for the sporadic outings with Amy, and she doesn't have much support from the adults in her life.

Like Olivia's, many families have one or more members who need help, care and support on a daily basis. It could be one of the parents suffering from a mental health illness like depression (as in Olivia's mother's case) or from a physical condition such as lupus or cancer. In other cases, one of the grandparents who lives at home with the family may suffer from dementia. It could also be that one of the children in the family is suffering from a developmental disorder like autism or another illness. There are also children who live with adults who suffer from alcohol or drug addiction. All these children often carry out a lot of caring tasks that are excessive for their age. The truth is that there are many serious illnesses and people who suffer from them need a high level of attention and care from another person who is in a better state physically and mentally, even if that person is a child. When a member of the family suffers from a chronic illness, drug or alcohol abuse, or a physical or mental condition, the whole family dynamic is affected, and all members of the family see their life changed by the circumstances.

These children or young adults who take on a caring role to look after someone in their family are called young carers. Looking more extensively into a complete theoretical definition of the term young carers, Becker explains that young carers are:

> children and young persons under 18 who provide or intend to provide care, assistance, or support to another family member. They carry out, often on a regular basis, significant, substantial caring tasks and assume a level of responsibility which would usually be associated with an adult. The person receiving care is often a parent but can be a sibling, grandparent, or other relative who is disabled, has some chronic illness, mental health problem or other condition connected with a need for care, support, or supervision.
>
> Becker (2000, p. 378)

Some other young carer definitions include young adult carers up to the age of 25; for example, The Carers Trust (2022):

> A young carer is someone aged 25 and under who cares for a friend or family member who, due to illness, disability, a mental health problem or an addiction, cannot cope without their support. Older young carers are also known as young adult carers and they may have different support needs to younger carers.

It is important to underline that, as Becker (2008) pointed out, there are cases where even if a child lives in a family where one member is ill, they might not become a young carer. These cases happen when there is plenty of support available, such as adult family members living in the household and undertaking most of the caring responsibilities, external support from different organisations, low severity of the illness, and so on. These children will, of course, also be affected by the fact of growing up with a member of the family who is in need of care, but the impact will not be as significant as that suffered by young carers who are sole carers with very little to no support. Overall, the impact of the caring role will be different for each young carer, depending on their individual situation. Variables as mentioned above, such as the severity of the illness of the care receiver, the personality of the young carer, the extent of care provided by the young carer, if there are other adult family members providing care, cultural and contextual factors, and so on, will play a significant role in the positive and negative impact that each young carer perceives from their caring role.

In this regard, Family Action (2012) states that:

> A young carer becomes vulnerable when the level of care-giving and responsibility to the person in need of care becomes excessive or inappropriate for that child risking impact on his or her emotional or physical wellbeing or educational achievement and life chances.

Some of the caring tasks that young carers undertake on a regular basis can include providing emotional support, administering drugs, helping with household chores, helping with mobility, cooking, budgeting, grocery shopping, taking care of financial duties, helping their relatives with personal hygiene, and so on.

For many years, the focus of the services provided was on helping to support the member of the family in need of care.

It has been assumed that this support would indirectly help the other members of the family, including the main carer, but has failed to consider that as they are still children, young carers may require specific services designed to meet their own needs.

However, in the past four decades, there has been a growing interest in studying and addressing the needs of young carers in several countries. The United Kingdom is one of the countries that has made great strides in this direction, promoting research in the area as well as in the design and implementation of specific services to address these carers' needs.

These children and young adults are often forced by circumstances to mature relatively early and hence miss out on important aspects of their childhood such as educational and recreational opportunities. Additionally, the overload of responsibilities and emotional involvement that their caring role requires will have an impact in several areas of their development and future life.

The general lack of awareness within families, schools and professional and health services of the impact of the caring role in childhood and young adult life has been making it difficult to identify and support these children and young adults. Furthermore, young carers are frequently unwilling to disclose their situation, as they often fear that they will be taken away from their family, that they will be ridiculed or bullied, or that their family will feel betrayed. Instead, they try to survive but feeling lonely and isolated in many cases, and often facing very stressful situations. The young carers' reluctance to disclose their situation further contributes to the 'invisibility' of this population and reduces efforts towards specific service provision.

Movements to support young carers started over 40 years ago at different levels in different countries. The UK has been the country where most change has been witnessed in this area. The Princess Royal Trust for Carers and Crossroads Care were some of the first organisations to fight for the rights of the young carers in the UK. Several changes have taken place in the past four decades that favour young carers in the UK. Changes in legislation and service provision have been some of the most important achievements. For instance, The Carers (Recognition & Services) Act 1995 and the Carers and Disabled Children Act (2000) both require that all informal carers (including young carers) who provide regular care are assessed and supported in their local area. Additionally, young carers projects have been established throughout the country, with the intention of raising awareness and providing support to these young people. Other countries such as Australia, New Zealand, Canada, and some European countries like Germany, Austria and Switzerland also have started efforts to identify, assess and support the young carers. An important project was also launched in the past years called is Me-We.Eu which aims to systemise knowledge about young carers, implementing a support system for these children in six countries (Sweden, Slovenia, Italy, the Netherlands, Switzerland and the UK) and to share internationally actionable knowledge on what has worked in order to help and support young carers.

In this book, we'll look closely at the impact that looking after a member of the family who is ill and/or dependent on care has on children. Although caring has been shown to have a positive impact on the lives of children, such as by building resilience and empathy and being more compassionate (Aldridge & Becker, 1993), other studies have also consistently shown that it has negative aspects that, if not considered and addressed adequately, can massively impact young carers. Let's dive into it.

Chapter Two

From Shadows to Spotlight: Research Reveals the Young Carer's Reality

As it was noted in the previous chapter, each young carer will live his or her caring role in a particular way. Although there is no universal agreement on what the positive and negative effects of being a young carer are, the last 40 years have seen some focus on gaining a better understanding in this field. The research utilised throughout this chapter largely originates from the UK and will also include notes and quotes from my own practice as a psychologist working with young carers. It is not my intention to give an extensive and detailed analysis of all the research that has been conducted in this field, but more an overview so that you can get a better idea of what struggles young carers face on a daily basis. It is important to remember, as mentioned in chapter one, that not all young carers will experience the same difficulties, it will all depend on their personal circumstances. The impact that the caring role can potentially have in the lives of young carers will be divided into five main areas in this chapter: positive impact, impact on school performance, psychological and emotional functioning, social impact, and physical impact.

Positive Impact of The Caring Role

Many studies have looked at the negative effects of being a young carer, but some researchers have also found that caring for a family member can have positive effects on the young carer. For instance, Dearden, Aldridge & Horwath (2010) found that young carers often become more mature, responsible, and independent, and they develop important life skills. They also gain a better understanding about disability issues, and their family relationships may become stronger when compared with their peers who are not young carers. Let's take a closer look at these positive effects.

I have personally noticed through my own work how the young carers more often than not tend to develop very strong relationships with the person that they care for. The extent of time that they are forced to spend with the family member in need of care is in many cases much greater than the time that some of their peers spend with their family. Olivia, for example, goes home straight after school every day to help her mother while some of her school friends go out together for some after-school activities. In many cases young carers are also aware of the dependence that the care seeker has on them – this also can help this relationship to strengthen. Young carers often feel proud of themselves as they perform their caring role and become aware of how useful they are and what an impact they are making in the life of the person they are caring for.

Additionally, it seems to have a very positive impact on the young carers when they receive appreciation and recognition for the job that they do: they feel useful and valued and this helps improve their self-esteem (Bolas et al., 2007). In this same line of findings Berardini et al., (2021) stated that through the compassion acts that they display while caring for their family member, young carers improve their self-esteem. The authors also found that compassion was likewise a factor that helped young carers develop positive regard for other people.

Research has also found that young carers tend to report higher levels of empathy than their peers which seems to help improve their mental well-being and moderate the potential negative impact of their caring role (Wepf et al., 2022). Young carers in my practice have often proved to be very generous, kind and altruistic towards their own family but also towards others and the community in general.

Young carers might also develop, in many cases, independent and practical life skills while performing their caring role (Dearden and Becker, 2000). Some of the caring tasks that young carers often perform – such as budgeting, cooking and planning – can be of great use during their adult life. These children and young people in many cases learn these skills before other children of the same age.

One more positive aspect that young carers often gain from their caring role is that they are in many cases very knowledgeable on specific medical conditions, normally on the ones that their family member is suffering from. Many young carers accompany their family members to doctors' appointments and are present during nurse visits at home. They also learn about the illness that their relative is suffering from during these meetings.

Finally, young carers also seem to mature faster than their peers in many cases (Banks et al., 2002). From an early age, these children and young adults are undertaking tasks and responsibilities that would normally belong to an adult. This forces them to mature faster than other children their age and they learn to take on responsibility really well. Olivia, for example, is behaving in a very mature way for her age by having to take care of her house and her family. She does tasks like cleaning the house, preparing meals and taking her brother to school, which other children her age don't regularly do.

Impact on School Performance

Many young carers are likely to see their academic performance affected. As an example Yeandle et al., (2007) found that young carers often are late to school, have difficulties in completing schoolwork on time, struggle to interact with other children at school, experience bullying and are likely to leave education without formal qualifications. Szafran et al., (2016) pointed out that young carers are often more tired than their peers and this affects their level of concentration at school. Becker and Sempik (2018) also suggested that the caring role has a negative impact on education. In their online survey, they found that the young carers reported high levels of absenteeism related to their caring role. They also noted how this could reduce their chances of getting good grades and of accessing employment in the future. Marsden (1995) noted that young carers also often reported that anxiety and fatigue were affecting their academic performance, that they showed low attainment and that they had fewer opportunities than their peers to join extra-curricular activities.

As in Olivia's case, the responsibilities taken on by these children are often very time-consuming, reducing the time and energy they have available to dedicate to their education. These children usually wake up earlier than their peers to make sure they help with the morning routine and in many cases they also go to bed late the night before. In some cases it might take longer than expected to organise everything at home in the morning causing young carers to often arrive at school late. There might be times when the looked-after relative is so unwell that the young carer decides to stay at home and look after them instead of going to school, further increasing the rate of absenteeism and lessons missed at school that day. Additionally, the time that they dedicate to looking after their relatives also reduces the time that they have available to complete their homework and focus on their studies. Being constantly tired also can impact their ability to concentrate, and it could create anxiety as the young carer tries their best to achieve good results, but fails. All these factors can also impact the opportunity that the young carer might have to achieve good grades at school and perhaps lead them to abandon education early which could translate into lower chances of accessing the labour market and getting a good job.

During my professional experience, I have observed numerous cases where young carers expressed their overwhelming responsibilities in taking care of their family members and assisting with household chores. As a result, their schoolwork was often neglected until late at night when they were already exhausted. One child, who attended my individual counselling sessions, explained that he lacked a suitable environment for concentration at home. He shared, 'Even if I had the desire to study, it simply isn't possible amidst all the chaos.' Another client, now an adult but formerly a young carer, specifically mentioned that they had never received any encouragement to excel in school. Consequently, they abandoned their education as soon as they had the opportunity to do so.

All the factors described in the previous paragraphs can also contribute to low motivation among young carers at school. One of the children who attended my practice mentioned that education was never prioritised in their home, and they were never informed about its importance. However, many other young carers I worked with were well aware of the significance of education. They expressed concerns about their poor academic performance despite their efforts because they understood that low grades could affect their future job prospects.

Caring responsibilities can also limit the time young carers have to socialise with their school friends outside of school hours, potentially making it difficult for them to interact with peers during school time. Taking Olivia's case as an example, her peers often gather for sports and leisure activities after school. Unfortunately, Olivia misses out on these opportunities as she feels she needs to return home to care for her mother and brother immediately after school. Engaging in after-school activities helps school friends strengthen their relationships, but Olivia doesn't have a chance to enhance her relationships outside of school hours. Additionally, Olivia's mother has never interacted with other mothers at school, so when Olivia was younger, she didn't have the opportunity, like many of her peers, to participate in playdates or attend events such as birthday parties. Cree (2003) found that 35% of the young carers in her study expressed worries about lacking friends, and Frank (1995) noted that many young carers experienced isolation from their peers.

As mentioned at the beginning of this chapter, many young carers also endure bullying at school. Dearden & Becker (2000) pointed out that young carers sometimes become targets of bullying due to their differences. These differences can arise from having more responsibilities at home compared with their peers or having a family member who is considered 'different' in some way. According to these authors, it is not the caregiving role itself that leads to bullying, but the distinct family situation. In many cases, bullying directed towards young carers involves insults and derogatory comments about their relatives, as seen in Olivia's case when she overheard friends saying negative things about her mother.

One of the young carers who attended my counselling sessions suffered greatly from the bullying he experienced at school. His peers constantly ridiculed him, calling him 'retarded' which was a reference to his brother who had autism. They would also bully his younger brother whenever they saw him in the playground. My client was constantly worried and distressed, not only about the bullying he endured but also about his brother being targeted by the bullies. Unfortunately, many children face bullying at school, and in the case of young carers, along with the stigma surrounding certain illnesses and the lack of awareness about their circumstances, bullying exacerbates their daily challenges.

Another issue young carers face at school is being reprimanded by teachers. Some studies have indicated that young carers sometimes feel punished by teachers for issues related to their caregiving responsibilities (Family Action, 2012). Becker (2019) further discovered that young carers were often confronted by teachers in front of their peers and asked to explain themselves publicly. These situations cause the children to feel embarrassed and distressed.

I also encountered similar situations with some of the young carers I worked with, particularly when teachers lacked awareness about the difficulties these children faced at home. They would be scolded for being late or absent or for not completing their homework. However, throughout my experience, young carers rarely confided in anyone at school about their home situation. They were afraid of being ridiculed, especially those who cared for relatives with mental health issues. One of the children said, 'I wouldn't expect any kind of help even if I disclosed what is going on at home.'

Impact on Emotional and Psychological Functioning

Research has consistently shown that young carers are exposed to higher risks of emotional and psychological struggles. Extensive research in this area has led to strong consensus on certain findings across different studies. However, it is important to recognise that the effects of the caring role on emotional and psychological functioning can vary significantly in each particular case. Several variables, such as the severity of the illness or the available support, as discussed earlier in this book, will influence how the young carer is affected by their caring role. Some young carers may experience a substantial impact on their emotional and psychological well-being, while others may experience milder effects or even none at all.

Having said that, there is already progress in this area and plenty of research has been carried out. Below are some relevant findings:

- Young carers often experience feelings of anger, anxiety, frustration, stress, resentment and guilt (Frank, 1995).
- Low self-esteem and depression are often experienced by young carers (Dearden & Becker, 1998; Frank et al., 1999; Dearden & Becker, 2000; Armstrong, 2002).
- A high number of young carers had reported mental health problems such as eating disorders and self-harm (Aldridge & Becker, 2003; Dearden & Becker, 2004).
- Children of parents with mental health issues recalled in their adulthood having had a childhood of isolation and abandonment and that their needs were always secondary to others' needs (McCormack et al., 2017).
- Adults who had a mentally ill parent during their childhood recalled having experienced high levels of abuse and neglect as a child (Dunn, 1993).
- Children caring for a parent with mental health issues are at higher risk of developing emotional and mental health disorders (Dharampal & Ani, 2020).
- Young carers experience real problems ranging from less serious ones like difficulties with sleeping and eating to more severe ones like self-harm and suicide attempts (Cree, 2003).

Understanding the mechanisms involved in the emotional and psychological difficulties experienced by young carers is a complex task, as there is limited scientific data to establish definitive causality links. Nonetheless, we can examine how the experiences young carers face in their daily lives may potentially affect their emotional and psychological well-being.

Consider Olivia's case. When her mother is depressed, Olivia feels an overwhelming sense of sadness and helplessness. She grapples with the reasons behind her mother's unhappiness and struggles to accept her mother's mental illness. Feelings of denial, anger, guilt and other emotions may arise in young carers like Olivia. Failure to process, integrate and accept these emotions can lead to more profound emotional and psychological difficulties and, unfortunately, many young carers do not receive the necessary support to cope with these feelings in a healthy way.

Many young carers, similar to Olivia, have witnessed and had to assist their family members during crises, such as aggressive or psychotic episodes or suicide attempts. Without an opportunity to process these experiences, the emotional and psychological development of the child is likely to be negatively affected.

Living in chaotic and unpredictable family dynamics, particularly when a parent suffers from mental health issues or substance abuse, can also impact a young carer's sense of safety and increase distress levels.

The overwhelming responsibilities placed on these children's shoulders, which are often excessive for their age, can also trigger emotional and psychological issues.

When young carers care for an ill parent, the roles are frequently reversed, and the child assumes tasks typically reserved for parents. This role reversal can disrupt the child's regular emotional and psychological development. Firstly, the child may have a less available parent to provide appropriate care. Secondly, they may be forced to mature earlier than their peers due to the emotional care they have to provide to the care recipient.

Moreover, young carers are frequently burdened with constant worries. Research by Thomas et al., (2003) revealed that many young carers reported feelings of sadness, and worries about various aspects of their lives, including the person they are caring for, academic performance, social interactions, feeling different from others, their future and family finances. These worries can contribute to higher levels of anxiety and reduced self-esteem.

As a psychologist working with young carers, I have consistently found that they recognise the emotional and psychological impact of their caring role. Many young carers expressed feelings of constant worry, sadness and loneliness. They often felt the need to mature quickly, and the distress caused by their perpetual concerns was particularly significant when caring for relatives with severe mental health issues.

Clearly, many young carers could benefit from professional psychological support. Unfortunately, as mentioned by Cree (2003), these young carers in need of help often go unnoticed by mental health professionals. The lack of awareness about young carers within society and the reluctance of these children to disclose their situations pose significant obstacles that must be addressed.

Impact on Social Life and Leisure Opportunities

Although we have already touched upon how being a young carer affects the social life of these children, it is essential to delve into this aspect further to gain a more comprehensive understanding.

For most children, free time is a given, and they can spend it as they please. They may choose to play alone or with friends, watch TV or engage in sports. Older children often go out with friends and participate in various activities. However, young carers often lack these choices; they are obliged to stay home and provide help.

Thomas et al., (2003) emphasised the importance of socialising for children and young people. This is particularly relevant for young carers, as spending time with friends outside the home can provide a much-needed break from the challenges they face at home. Unfortunately, young carers have significantly fewer opportunities than their peers to socialise due to their caregiving responsibilities.

Based on my own experience, young carers frequently express that they have less leisure time and fewer chances for recreational activities compared with their peers. Many have never experienced a family day out. They often lack opportunities to engage in fun activities independently or play with friends. One young carer I worked with said, 'I never got to do things I liked just for fun.' Moreover, some young carers who do have a group of friends may still feel somewhat disconnected and perceive themselves as 'different'.

Due to the lack of opportunities to socialise with peers, young carers often feel isolated and socially excluded. This can lead to difficulties in making friends and maintaining relationships both in childhood and adulthood (Crabtree & Warner, 1999). They worry about not having friends and what other children might think of them. Additionally, they may believe that others do not understand why they cannot go out more often.

As mentioned earlier, young carers are at a higher risk of being bullied at school compared with other children. Aldridge & Becker (2003) suggest that this risk is more prevalent among those caring for someone with a mental illness or substance abuse due to the lack of understanding and persisting stigma surrounding these conditions.

The limited opportunities for socialising and engaging in age-appropriate fun activities contribute to the emotional, social and educational impact on young carers' development. The resulting isolation and social exclusion can potentially lead to short-term and long-term challenges in these areas of their lives.

Physical Impact

The caring role can have various physical impacts on young carers, which may be influenced by the nature of their family member's illness. Young carers who support a family member with mobility challenges may be more affected physically than those caring for someone who is physically self-sufficient.

In a study by Becker (2019), many young carers reported assisting their relatives with mobility, involving tasks such as lifting and helping them up and down stairs. As a result, some young carers experienced physical issues like back pain. Hill (1999) also noted that these physical efforts could lead to lasting back problems in adulthood.

Even if they care for a physically self-sufficient family member, young carers may still experience physical impacts from their caring role. For instance, they may face sleep deprivation due to their caring responsibilities (Noble-Carr, 2002). In some cases, they might suffer from poor nutrition as they are left to plan and prepare meals without adequate support, leading them to opt for quick and easy but less nutritious options. Additionally, as pointed out by Barber & Siskowski (2008), some young carers may be deprived of proper paediatric care, often due to neglect, limited financial resources, or a lack of parental responsibility.

Throughout this chapter, we have seen that the outcomes of being a young carer can have severe negative impacts, especially if the young carer lacks support in their role. In the following chapters, we will explore some top-line ideas on how to help these children and young people cope with these challenges and negative consequences.

Chapter Three

Empowerment Tools for Young Carers

Whether you're a young carer looking for ways to manage your responsibilities or someone who wants to support a young carer, such as a family member, friend or teacher, this section offers practical ideas and friendly advice. Even if you're not a young carer yourself, you can still learn from the tips below and share them with someone you want to help.

Keep in mind that the suggestions provided here aren't a one-size-fits-all solution to instantly solve the challenges young carers face every day. I've drawn from my experience working with young carers, and while these ideas have helped many, they might vary in effectiveness from person to person. Some young carers might find all the advice valuable, others might find a few tips useful, and some might not relate to this chapter at all. Remember, it's up to you to decide what advice to try, if any. It's understandable that you might feel that adding these suggestions to your already busy life is overwhelming. Taking things step by step is always recommended. Each small step matters and should contribute to feeling a bit better.

On a different note, some young carers might think that the advice in this chapter seems a bit selfish, like seeking respite, which involves sharing caregiving duties with someone else for a short time, or prioritising 'me time'. If you (or the young carer you're supporting) feel this way, remember (or remind them) that taking care of yourself ultimately benefits your loved ones too. When you're in good physical and emotional shape, you'll have more energy and be in a better mood to provide effective support.

If you're helping a young carer who is very young and still learning to read and write, you can adjust the advice below and explain it in simpler terms. Some of the self-help suggestions might not be suitable for younger children, who might need different types of assistance.

Always remember that any effort you put into self-help and self-care will contribute to improving your overall well-being, both mentally and physically. Your well-being matters, and these suggestions are here to support you in your journey.

Tell People You Trust About Your Situation

At times, you might feel anxious about discussing your situation with others, fearing potential consequences like involving social services and being separated from your family. However, keeping concerns to oneself and avoiding seeking help can lead to missed opportunities for support and increased difficulties.

Speaking to someone you trust can make a significant difference. This person could be an adult like a parent, an aunt or uncle, a teacher at school, or even a friend, sibling, cousin or anyone with whom you feel comfortable sharing. Having a list of trusted contacts ready for tough moments can be beneficial (Annex 1). Whether face to face, over the phone, by text message, or email, communicating with a trusted individual is vital. Sharing emotions and thoughts with them is a way of taking control and seeking assistance actively.

Some young carers might find it challenging to discuss their caregiving role due to its personal nature. Sharing what's happening at home can feel overwhelming, causing shyness, embarrassment, or a sense of betrayal towards the person they care for. If this resonates with you, here are some tips that might help:

1. **Remember that there's no reason to be ashamed.** Your efforts in supporting your relatives are commendable and something to take pride in. You're not betraying them; you're seeking ways to better manage your caregiving role.
2. **Choose a suitable, calm time** to talk to the person you wish to confide in. Find a moment when they're not rushed and can listen attentively. If possible, arrange the meeting in advance, highlighting the importance of what you want to share.
3. **Plan the conversation ahead of time.** Consider what you want to say and in what sequence. Writing down your thoughts could ease stress during the actual conversation. Remember, while sharing feelings and experiences is meant to reduce anxiety and provide support, the decision to share and the extent of sharing are entirely yours. If there's something you're not comfortable sharing or aren't ready for, that's perfectly okay. You might be ready in the future, or perhaps not, but the key is knowing you have someone willing to listen if you choose to share.

Inform Yourself

Take the time to learn about the illness your relative is facing. Nowadays, information is readily accessible through books, the internet, or by asking an adult for guidance. Any method of gathering information is valid, and understanding more about the illness can greatly improve your insight into the situation.

For instance, you might sometimes feel frustrated by your relative's actions or reactions, or by their inability to perform certain tasks. By learning about why the illness can lead to such behaviour, you can find it easier to provide support and experience less stress or frustration when they exhibit these behaviours. This understanding helps you grasp what your relative is going through due to their illness.

Creating a list of the most common symptoms your relative displays (Annex 2) is a useful step. This allows you to pinpoint ways to manage these symptoms or behaviours as they arise. For example, if your relative is dealing with depression, there might be days when they feel incredibly sad and cry frequently. Such situations can affect your emotions as well. To prepare for these moments, consider activities that can lift your mood, like going for a walk, talking to a friend, focusing on calming thoughts, or any activity that brings you comfort and positivity. This proactive approach can contribute to helping you feel better during challenging times.

Prepare an Emergency Plan

Prepare an emergency plan in case your relative experiences a crisis (Annex 3).

Gather Relevant Information About Your Relative's Illness or Condition

Begin by jotting down any essential details about your relative's illness. This could include the specific condition they're dealing with, contact information for their GP, psychologist, or any other professional involved in their care. If you're aware of the medications and dosages they're taking, it's beneficial to note these down as well. While you're not obligated to know all these particulars, having them written down can be valuable. Remember, it's absolutely fine if you don't have all this information, but if you do, keeping it accessible can prove helpful.

Compile Emergency Contact Numbers

Write down the emergency service numbers like ambulance, childline support, 999 or 112 specific to your area. Additionally, include the contact details of any individuals you trust and who could be of assistance during an emergency. Through my work with young carers, I've encountered instances where identifying trustworthy individuals during emergencies posed challenges. If this resonates with you, don't worry. Understand that professional emergency services are available to help during critical situations. Being unable to pinpoint someone to trust for help isn't your fault, and this situation can evolve as you establish relationships with new people or strengthen existing connections.

Inform Trusted Individuals

If you've identified reliable individuals and included their contact information in your list, make sure to inform them. This way, they'll be aware in advance that you might reach out to them for assistance during an emergency involving your relative.

In the Event of an Emergency

If an emergency occurs, dial the emergency services and contact a trusted person if they're listed in your plan. Share the information you've compiled to provide a comprehensive picture of the situation.

Creating an emergency plan not only proves invaluable during critical times but also alleviates your worries because you know that you have a well-thought-out course of action if an emergency arises.

Respite – Identify Helpers

Recognise individuals in your life who are close to you and willing to provide assistance on occasion (Annex 4). They might be able to step in and supervise your family member while you take some personal time, or lend a hand with household chores and grocery shopping. These individuals could be family members, friends, neighbours – anyone whom you trust and believe would be open to helping when needed. This group might include the same people you identified for your emergency plan, or you could consider other options.

If you find it challenging to come up with potential helpers, remember that this isn't your fault. As we discussed earlier while crafting the emergency plan, each young carer's situation is unique, and there are circumstances where trusted individuals might be scarce in a your circle of relationships. If this applies to you, don't worry. There are cases where support services are available in your local area, and we'll delve into these later in this chapter.

In case you manage to identify individuals who are willing to lend a hand from time to time, it's incredibly beneficial to establish a schedule ahead of time. Note down which days and hours they could assist you. This way, if you like, you can also plan in advance how you'll use that free time. This organised approach not only helps in managing your responsibilities but also allows you to make the most of your time to recharge.

Ask For Help Services In Your Local Area

The awareness of young carers' needs varies significantly from country to country. It's worth taking the time to research the available services in your local area. In some countries, like the UK, there are well-developed local support groups for young carers. If you don't have easy access to research tools like the internet, consider asking a teacher or a GP for guidance. Even if official help services aren't present in your area, these professionals can still be of great assistance. School counsellors, teachers, doctors, social workers and others are likely to offer valuable help to young carers (Annex 5).

Most schools have counsellors. Even if the school isn't fully aware of your needs, a counsellor can be a valuable resource. They can provide support during tough times and suggest coping strategies to help you manage better. It's important to note that counsellors usually maintain confidentiality policies. This means you can talk to them without worrying about them sharing your information without your consent. Some counsellors might propose discussing your situation with teachers to increase awareness, but they would typically seek your permission before sharing any information. You can work out with the counsellor what details you're comfortable sharing with your teachers. During your first meeting, the counsellor will likely explain the specifics of confidentiality. While confidentiality is usually maintained, there are exceptions. For instance, a counsellor might breach confidentiality if they have serious concerns about your safety or someone else's. They should provide all the details about confidentiality, but if they don't, feel free to ask for clarification.

Look After Yourself

Take Care of Your Physical Well-being

Ensure that you're taking care of yourself physically. Prioritise eating well, staying hydrated and exercising whenever possible. Based on my personal experience working with young carers, it's common for them to get caught up in assisting their family members, often neglecting their own meals, forgetting to drink water regularly, and struggling to find time for exercise. Maintaining good physical health is essential for better emotional and psychological coping with your role as a young carer.

Make Time for Yourself

Even if your situation is more challenging compared with other kids your age, strive to set aside time just for yourself. This can involve watching your favourite TV series or engaging in activities you truly enjoy. Aim to incorporate this 'me time' as frequently as possible. You can also include the time you've agreed upon for rest when others will look after your relative (respite helpers). Identify moments when your relative requires less attention – such as when their condition goes through a more manageable phase – and plan ahead to seize that time. Additionally, if your relative goes to bed early, consider utilising the free time that follows.

Prioritise Your Emotional Well-being

Focusing on your emotional well-being is crucial. As discussed in the second chapter, research reveals that being a young carer can trigger a wide range of emotions, some of which are intensified compared to children without caregiving responsibilities. While there are positive emotions tied to caregiving, like a sense of closeness to the person you're caring for, negative feelings such as anger, frustration and isolation are also common. It's perfectly normal to experience a mix of emotions in this role, and it's important to remember that you should never blame yourself for how you feel. Allow your feelings to exist and accept them as valid.

From my interactions with young carers, I've observed how extended family members sometimes unfairly place the entire caregiving responsibility on the young carer. In some cases, they may even unjustly blame you when things don't go as planned. It's crucial to understand that you're still a child and, no matter what, no one has the right to hold you solely accountable for your relative's care. Ensuring your well-being and meeting your needs is a shared responsibility. Therefore, be aware of such comments and don't let them burden you emotionally. Be kind to yourself, because you deserve it.

Everyone experiences negative thoughts and emotions daily. These thoughts might be more prevalent among young carers, given the higher stress levels and greater responsibilities they face compared to their peers. While negative thoughts and emotions are a natural part of life, finding strategies to cope with them is key. Our emotions stem from our thoughts, so working towards positive thinking or memories can lead to more positive emotions. Even small shifts from negative to positive thinking on a daily basis can improve your overall well-being.

A few techniques that can help are:

1. Positive Thinking

   Identify thoughts or memories that bring you joy. These could be thoughts of singing a favourite song in your head or recalling a calming moment by the sea. Others might prefer to remember positive achievements or moments with loved ones.

Dedicate time to focus on your positive thoughts. Spend a few minutes each morning after waking up strongly dwelling on that positive thought. You can do this while lying in bed and taking deep breaths, or at a time that suits you.

Recognise negative emotions. Pay attention to when emotions like anger, sadness, fear, frustration, loneliness, guilt or resentment arise.

Bring your identified positive thought or memory to mind. Concentrate on it for a couple of minutes, allowing the intensity of the negative emotion to decrease.

2. Write Down Feelings And Emotions

Writing down your experiences, feelings and emotions can also be helpful. Keeping a journal and regularly recording your thoughts can lead to a better understanding of what's happening in your life. Putting your experiences into words can help unveil emotions that might otherwise remain abstract. By translating these emotions into written form, you externalise them, decluttering your mind, which might be overwhelmed by thoughts and emotions that you hesitate to share with others. Writing daily also organises your experiences chronologically, leading to greater insight and allowing you to divert energy from trying to understand your feelings towards focusing on new things.

3. Gratitude Journal

Another simple technique that enhances overall emotional well-being is maintaining a gratitude journal. Every day before bed (or at a convenient time), write down five positive things that happened to you that day (Annex 6). These could be simple things you're grateful for. For instance:

- I had my favourite meal today for lunch (pasta carbonara).
- I spent quality time with my best friend.
- My mother was in a good mood today.
- I finished my homework quickly.
- The weather was lovely, and I enjoyed the sunny walk to school.

This exercise fosters a positive mindset and can even improve sleep by reducing negative emotions, as mentioned earlier.

In closing this section, just remember that by reading this book and implementing the advice shared here, you're already taking steps to care for yourself. Congratulations!

Resources for Self-Help

Self-care app: https://apps.apple.com/gb/app/young-carers-support-app/id1556955591

Young carers support website: https://me-we.eu/

1. Annex 1. List of Trusted People
2. Annex 2. List of Symptoms
3. Annex 3. Emergency Plan
   a. Information about relative and their condition: name, surname, illness, details to doctors or any professional service that is helping
   b. Numbers of emergency services/ Numbers of trusted people
4. Annex 4. Respite Plan
   a. Respite helpers: Name and contact number
   b. Monthly schedule for respite rests
5. Annex 5. List of Help Services in the Area
6. Annex 6. Diary of Positive Things

Name	Relationship	Mobile Number	Email	Address

Symptoms

Symptom / Behaviour	How I feel	How could I feel better

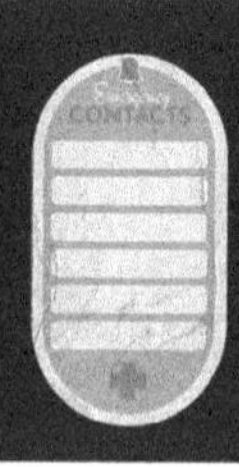

Emergency Plan

Young carer's details	
Name and surname:	
Date of birth:	
Mobile:	
Email:	
Address:	

Details of person cared for	
Name and surname:	
Date of birth:	
Mobile:	
Email:	
Address:	

Medical condition of person cared for	
Medical condition:	
Medication:	
Allergies:	
Tricks to help her/him calm down:	
Name and telephone number of GP:	
Health center name where the GP practises:	
Name and telephone number of psychologist	
Name and telephone number of psychiatrist:	
Name and telephone number of social worker:	

Additional information the young carer considers relevant

Emergency services contact details	
National emergency response service:	
Health emergency services:	
Ambulance:	
Police:	
Fire services:	

Details of trusted people to contact in emergencies	
Contact 1: Name & surname, mobile, email, address, relationship to the young carer.	
Contact 2: Name & surname, mobile, email, address, relationship to the young carer.	
Contact 3: Name & surname, mobile, email, address, relationship to the young carer.	

Respite Plan

Respite Helpers		
Name and surname	**Contact number**	**Respite day and time**

Help Services

Service Name	Address	Contact Number

Positive Thoughts

Positive thought	Emotion felt

Chapter Four

Establishing Support Systems for Young Carers in Schools

In this chapter, I'll provide a concise guide on how schools and education professionals can establish a support network for young carers. While the UK is notably advanced in this area, other countries can benefit from similar approaches. Drawing from my experience supporting young carers in a London school, I'll offer advice based on both research and practical insights. At the chapter's conclusion, I'll list online resources available in the UK, which can serve as a guide for other nations.

Authors have noted that schools and their staff are well-positioned to identify young carers (Thomas et al., 2003). Teachers and school staff interact with young carers daily. If they recognise the signs, they can identify these children and offer them support. Mortimore (1995) adds that schools often serve as a protective factor for distressed children, providing the routine and security they might lack at home. Thus, schools play a crucial role in identifying and supporting young carers, enhancing the protective role they already have.

Schools will have distinct policies and procedures, influencing their approach to young carer support. Additionally, different countries have varying policies regarding young carers, which may impact how schools address their needs.

Setting Up Support in Schools for Young Carers – Top-line Guide

Designate a Person or Team for Young Carer Support

Select a staff member or group interested in the topic and willing to dedicate time to comprehend it comprehensively. If a team is assigned, nominate one member as the young carer's lead – a central contact for matters related to young carers. After receiving education on the topic, the designated person/team can begin creating an action plan to develop the school's young carer support system.

Create Awareness Material

Create material to educate staff, students and parents about young carers, their challenges, and how to support them:

- Compile a clear definition of 'young carer' and explain the impact of caregiving on children and young adults. Share this with staff first, and later with students and parents.
- Distribute information through leaflets, workshops, assemblies, videos and talks from external speakers. Schools can use available information on the topic, including content from this book.
- Prioritise raising awareness among staff before students and parents. Establish an initial support system for young carers within the school staff before proceeding.

Create an Identification Process

Identifying young carers can be challenging, especially when awareness is just beginning. Young carers might be hesitant to seek support in school due to various reasons, such as:

1. **Fear of Separation:** worries about being placed into care and separated from their family if authorities discover their family situation.
2. **Lack of Self-Awareness:** not recognising their own role as a carer.
3. **Limited Opportunity to Share:** lack of chances to express their experiences.
4. **Lack of Trust:** distrust in the school's ability to provide support.
5. **Embarrassment:** feeling embarrassed about their family situation.
6. **Fear of Standing Out:** worrying about being different from their peers.

To address young carers' reluctance to share their situation, professionals must demonstrate awareness of their concerns and provide reassurance.

Use Checklists for Identification

Employing a checklist can be a helpful initial tool for identifying young carers in school. This checklist can be shared with students, families, teachers and staff. Below are examples of checklists for students and their families, as well as one for teachers and school staff. Keep in mind that while many students might relate to some statements, a young carer will be able to relate to multiple statements. The checklist is an illustrative guide and not an official assessment tool.

Top-line Checklist for Students and Families (Initial Identification)

A young carer is a child or young adult who has a family member of any age with a: (a young carer will tick at least one of the items from the 5 below)

- ☐ Long-term illness or condition (for example – cancer, Alzheimer's, heart disease, diabetes, etc)
- ☐ Mental health problem (for example – depression, bipolar disorder, schizophrenia, anxiety disorder, etc)
- ☐ Physical disability (for example – multiple sclerosis, conditions like tetraplejia causing mobility impairments, etc)
- ☐ Developmental disability (for example – autism, Down syndrome, cerebral palsy, etc)
- ☐ Addiction problems (for example – alcoholism, drugs, etc)

Might have to do some of the below jobs:

- ☐ Spend a lot of time doing house duties like vacuuming, doing laundry, cleaning dishes, etc
- ☐ Cooking
- ☐ Doing the grocery shopping
- ☐ Helping their relative with moving from place to place
- ☐ Helping their relative with personal hygiene like showers
- ☐ Helping their relative get dressed
- ☐ Helping their relative go to the toilet
- ☐ Helping their relative in emergency situations
- ☐ Talking to their relative to cheer them up
- ☐ Helping their relative to calm down
- ☐ Going to the doctor with their relative
- ☐ Giving medicines to their relative
- ☐ Taking responsibility for a sibling
- ☐ Taking responsibility for the family finances

May be experiencing some of the below:

- ☐ Often worrying about their relative
- ☐ Feeling generally worried
- ☐ Feeling worried about the future
- ☐ Experiencing bullying at school
- ☐ Having to miss school or be late because of looking after their relative
- ☐ Having difficulties in completing homework
- ☐ Having difficulties in achieving good results at school
- ☐ Feeling frustrated, sad, angry, worried, stressed
- ☐ Feeling tired
- ☐ Feeling isolated
- ☐ Missing out on social activities like going out with their friends

Top-line checklist for teachers and school staff

A young carer in your class might present some of the below:

- ☐ Absenteeism
- ☐ Punctuality issues
- ☐ Problems with homework
- ☐ Performance issues (underachievement)
- ☐ Disturbed behaviour (withdrawn, angry)
- ☐ Constant need to be in contact with home
- ☐ Poor motivation
- ☐ Tiredness
- ☐ Poor contact with school from parents/guardian
- ☐ Poor hygiene/appearance
- ☐ Poor attention span
- ☐ Missing out in extra-curricular activities

- ☐ Being bullied
- ☐ Poor self-esteem
- ☐ Social isolation
- ☐ Higher levels of maturity compared to peers

Remember, every student's situation is unique, and these checklists offer a preliminary understanding. If you notice any student exhibiting several of these characteristics, consider initiating a conversation to better comprehend their circumstances. By fostering understanding and open communication, schools can create a supportive environment for young carers.

Create an Assessment Process

In-Depth Assessment of Young Carers' Needs: Using Questionnaires

To gain a comprehensive understanding of a young carer's situation and determine the most effective support, the young carers lead may conduct a more detailed assessment. This assessment can help gather detailed information on the following aspects:

1. **Relative and Condition:** identify the family member requiring care and their specific illness or condition.
2. **Level of Care Needed:** understand the extent of care required by the family member.
3. **Young Carer's Involvement:** determine the tasks the young carer performs and the time spent on caregiving.
4. **Support System:** assess whether the young carer receives support from family, friends or external agencies.
5. **Impact on Young Carer:** understand how caregiving affects the young carer emotionally, socially, academically and physically.

6. **Desired Support:** identify the types of support the young carer wishes to receive at school.

The young carer's team can utilise questionnaires to collect additional information on the young carer's needs and the best ways to support them. Joseph et al., (2009) developed these questionnaires, found in the Manual for Measures of Caring Activities and Outcomes for Children and Young People. This resource is accessible on the Carers Trust website in the UK: https://carers.org/resources/all-resources/101-manual-for-measures-of-caring-activities-and-outcomes-for-children-and-young-people.

This manual includes the following questionnaires:

1. **Multidimensional Assessment of Caring Activities (MACA) 18:** a quick and user-friendly questionnaire to be completed by young carers. It estimates the level of care the child or young person is providing. It also provides data on subscales like domestic tasks, household management, personal care, emotional care, sibling care, and financial/practical care.
2. **Positive and Negative Outcomes of Caring (PANOC) 20:** this questionnaire gauges the subjective positive and negative effects of the caregiving role as perceived by the young carer.

To enhance the assessment, the authors provide additional resources:

- **MACA YC42:** a more extensive version of the MACA 18 with 42 items. It offers a detailed insight into the young carer's caregiving level.
- **WHAT I LIKE AND DISLIKE ABOUT CARING:** this questionnaire delves into the young carer's emotions and feelings toward the caregiving role.

- **Post Intervention Self Assessment (PISA) CT2012:** this tool evaluates the young carer's opinions on the support received through an intervention.

Using these questionnaires can help schools and professionals gain a more accurate understanding of young carers' needs and preferences, allowing them to tailor their support effectively.

Create an Initial Support Model for Young Carers in the School

Creating a comprehensive support system for young carers is an ongoing process, but schools can start by providing initial support and gradually improving their services. Here are some steps that schools can take as a starting point:

- **Designate a Young Carers Contact Point:** the previously chosen young carers lead can serve as the main contact point for anyone with questions about young carers, including the young carers themselves.
- **Develop an Action Plan:** once awareness is raised among pupils and families, those identifying as young carers can contact the designated staff member. For ease and flexibility, they should be provided with various contact channels, such as phone, email, whatsapp, or in-person meetings. Parents or individuals who know the young carer can also approach the school's contact point on their behalf.

- **Initial Support Actions:**

  Training for teachers:
  Provide regular training for teachers to identify and support young carers in their classrooms. Some examples of immediate actions teachers can take in class without

confronting the young carer once they know one of their students is a young carer include the following:

- Foster a supportive environment in the classroom by being empathetic and flexible with their needs.
- Inform the young carers team or lead about the situation and seek advice.

Informative sessions:
Offer informative sessions to young carers and their families about research and available support.

Raise awareness:
Raise awareness about available support within the school.

Counselling:
Provide one-on-one counselling sessions for young carers.

Group support sessions:
Arrange weekly or monthly group support sessions for young carers to share experiences and build connections. These support sessions can have different content every week/month, for example:

- Information sessions
- Homework sessions
- Experience-sharing sessions
- Art sessions
- Resource-sharing sessions

External Support Services:

The young carer's lead can proactively identify potential support services to refer young carers to when needed. Depending on the country and locality, external support services can be referred to young carers in need:

- Look for young carer groups or other relevant support services in the community.
- Explore free counselling services for children in need.
- Utilise child support lines where children can seek professional help through calls, emails, or online chats.
- Investigate after-school activities and outings offered by various organisations.

It's important to recognise that building a support system takes time, and schools can continuously refine and enhance their services based on the evolving needs of young carers and their families.

Remember that each school's circumstances vary, so the approach might differ. Flexibility is key in tailoring these steps to suit your school's resources and policies. By prioritising young carer support, schools can play a vital role in enhancing the well-being of these dedicated individuals.

Resources for Schools

- https://youngcarersinschools.com/
- https://www.littledreamers.org.au/programs/the-young-carer-project/
- https://www.actionforcarers.org.uk/wp-content/uploads/2020/09/Young-Carers-Identification-Guide-a-tool-for-education-staff.pdf

Chapter Five

From NGOs to Communities: Backing Young Carers

Organisations focused on supporting young carers play a crucial role in providing tailored assistance and services to these individuals and their families. While the specifics of setting up and running such programmes may vary, here's a top-line guide on how organisations can support young carers and their families.

Raising Awareness

Organisations can spread awareness about their services through schools, health centres, social workers, TV, and various other communication channels to reach young carers and their families.

Referrals

Young carers can be referred to the organisation through various channels, including schools, health centres, and direct contact from young carers, or their family, friends, or other acquaintances.

Assessments

An assessment process can involve interviews with the young carer, parents/guardians and school tutors, and potentially home visits for families with mobility challenges.

Tailored Support Plans

Organisations typically develop personalised support plans based on the assessed needs of each young carer.

Services included in these plans can range from club activities to counselling and practical help. Some examples are listed below.

Young Carers Clubs

Young carers clubs offer the young carer a respite from their caring responsibilities, allowing them to have fun and form friendships with peers who share similar experiences. The activities organised provide a space for sharing, reducing isolation, boosting self-esteem and offering emotional support. These clubs provide regular activities and outings for young carers, fostering a supportive environment. Activities can include weekly sessions of arts and crafts, special food events, information sessions, and outings during weekends or school holidays.

Transport and Care Assistance

In some cases, organisations offer additional services to help young carers attend club activities. These services may include providing transportation or arranging a carer to assist the young carer's relative while they participate in the club.

Individual Support Services

Organisations offer one-on-one meetings to provide information, advice, guidance, and advocacy. Topics covered can range from community services and benefits to advocacy on behalf of the young carer.

Parenting Support

Organisations offer parenting support, helping parents/ guardians strengthen their skills and understand the impact of caring roles on their children.

Respite Services

Some organisations provide respite care by sending carers to look after the family member being cared for, allowing young carers to take a break.

Counselling and Therapies

One-to-one counselling, play therapy, art therapy and group therapy are often available for young carers to address their emotional and psychological needs.

Practical Training

Organisations may offer training sessions covering topics like moving and handling, first aid, emotional support techniques, and more.

It's important to note that the services offered may vary depending on the organisation's resources, expertise and national policies. The goal of these support systems is to provide young carers with a safe space, opportunities for personal growth, respite, and connections with peers who understand their unique challenges. Over time, organisations continuously adapt and expand their services to better meet the evolving needs of young carers and their families.

Chapter Six

Olivia's New Dawn: The Power of Support

Olivia's school had recently launched a support project for young carers. As part of this initiative, they designated a young carer's lead for any queries related to young carers. Additionally, they rolled out training programmes to educate teachers and staff about the unique challenges young carers face and the signs that might indicate a student is in such a role. The school also implemented an initial support system to assist these students once identified.

One day, Olivia was quietly pulled aside by her teacher for a private discussion. The compassion and understanding in the teacher's expression took Olivia by surprise, leaving her momentarily puzzled about the intent behind the meeting. The teacher began, 'Olivia, I've arranged this chat because I've observed certain patterns that made me want to reach out and see if there's any way I can assist you.' She noted Olivia's frequent tardiness, the occasional absences without medical reasons and the evident struggle with homework completion. 'I've also realised that you don't seem to have many friends and rarely participate in after-school activities,' she added gently. 'I want you to know this conversation isn't about judgement or pressuring you to improve. I genuinely want to help,' the teacher continued, expressing her wish for Olivia to confide in her, even if it concerned matters at home. 'I've noticed it's been challenging for the school to communicate with your mum about your progress. Is everything okay at home?' she inquired gently. She acknowledged the natural apprehension some students feel discussing family issues, understanding that many fear that exposing their household troubles could lead to interventions they might not want. 'There's a common concern,' the teacher said, 'where some children fear being taken away from their homes if authorities find out a parent is unwell or incapable of providing care.' Quickly, she transitioned into explaining the school's young carers' support initiative. 'Young carers,' she said, 'are children who shoulder the responsibility of caring for a family member with special care needs.' She outlined the resources available: confidential counselling sessions, a dedicated contact lead for young carers, and the assurance that any support extended would be with the child's full consent. 'I don't know if this is relevant to you,' she admitted, handing Olivia a leaflet. It provided a comprehensive overview of what 'young carer' meant, included a self-assessment checklist, and listed the contact information of the school's young carers lead. Olivia took a moment before responding, 'Thank you for your concern. I appreciate the information, but everything's fine at home. I'll focus on improving my punctuality and homework.'

While the school was aware of the tragic accident that had happened to Olivia's father, they remained oblivious to her mother's deepening depression and the consequent reliance on her children for support.

Returning home, Olivia's mind raced with the day's conversation. A persistent fear had always remained in her heart: the fear of being separated from her mum. In her eyes, if social services were to evaluate their situation, they might deem her mother unfit to care for her and Benjamin. Yet, amidst her anxiety, a hint of comfort emerged. The realisation that support was available if ever needed was reassuring. The term 'young carer' was unfamiliar to her, but as she read through the leaflet repeatedly, her understanding became clear. Completing the checklist, she began to tick the boxes. By the end, it was unmistakable – Olivia was a young carer.

A fortnight later, during a school assembly, the spotlight was on young carers. A detailed presentation was given about who they were, the responsibilities they shouldered at home, and the unique challenges they faced compared with their peers. Wrapping up the talk, a 16-year-old boy from a neighbouring school, a young carer for nine years, took the stage. With candid honesty, he shared his journey, detailing the uphill battles he faced. But, more importantly, he underscored the transformative difference the support at his school and the understanding of his peers made once they became aware of his role as a young carer.

One gloomy morning, Olivia woke up, feeling overwhelmed and sad. Coincidentally, it was another one of those days where Jane's depression anchored her to her bed. Throughout the day, the thought of seeking help incessantly circled Olivia's mind. By evening, she found herself drafting an email to the school's young carers lead. With heartfelt honesty, she detailed the challenges she faced caring for her unwell mother, her brother and their home. Her email echoed with anxiety — of being judged, of social services potentially intervening, of her family being torn apart. Confidentiality, she stressed, was crucial. She agonised over every word, every sentiment; the weight of sending the email bore heavily on her shoulders. Contemplating the consequences, both good and bad, she hesitated. But, after multiple reviews, she finally clicked 'send'. The next day, a storm of worry clouded Olivia's thoughts. She fretted about whether her email had been disseminated amongst the school staff, exposing her vulnerable family situation. Yet, the day unfolded without a hint of her secret being unveiled. Arriving home, she hurriedly checked her email, finding a response from the young carers lead, Tania. The email radiated warmth and understanding. Tania commended Olivia's courage in taking that pivotal first step, reaffirming the promise of confidentiality. She extended an invitation to Olivia, suggesting a face- to-face discussion to explore potential support options. However, recognising Olivia's apprehension, Tania also offered the alternative of continuing their conversation via email or WhatsApp until Olivia felt ready to talk face to face.

A week passed before Olivia gathered the courage to step into Tania's office. Her initial anxiety was palpable, but Tania's warm and empathetic presence quickly dispelled the nervous energy, allowing for an open dialogue. The conversation wandered through various facets of Olivia's life – her responsibilities at home, the toll they took on her, and the looming fears that overshadowed her daily existence. Among her concerns, the fear of being separated from her family topped the list, closely followed by the worry of her peers discovering her situation and making fun of her. As Tania continually reassured her and maintained an atmosphere of understanding, Olivia found herself diving deeper into her story. Midway, Tania introduced a detailed checklist designed to provide insight into the life of a young carer. It explored specifics such as the nature of the family member's condition, the support provided by the carer, and the resulting effects on their well-being. Completing it collaboratively, the exercise equipped Tania with a holistic view of Olivia's caregiving role and the implications it had on her life. Recognising that the duration of their conversation had considerably stretched, Tania gently steered it to a close, thinking it best not to overwhelm Olivia during their initial meet. They settled on a follow-up session two days later, with the goal of delving deeper into Olivia's circumstances and charting out potential support mechanisms. As they wrapped up, Tania reiterated her availability, assuring Olivia that she could reach out anytime, be it through WhatsApp, email, or in person.

In their next meeting, Tania found out more about Olivia's circumstances. It came to light that Olivia and her family operated in relative isolation, lacking any external support, whether institutional or familial. To further profile Olivia's caregiving situation and its ramifications, Tania introduced two structured assessments: the MACA YC42 and the PANOC 20. These tools provided Tania with nuanced insights, further refining her understanding of the challenges Olivia and her family faced. Afterwards, Tania outlined the support mechanisms the school had in place for young carers. This included weekly individual counselling sessions with Tania herself, and the initiation of a young carers support group that would convene bi-weekly at the school. This group would offer an environment to share experiences, engage in activities like arts and crafts, and even work on homework collectively. Olivia was surprised to learn there were several others like her within the school who had also reached out to Tania. She had always felt isolated in her experience. After some contemplation, Olivia decided to participate in the individual counselling sessions and also committed to joining the young carers support group when it started.

The counselling sessions soon became a therapeutic outlet for Olivia. While her responsibilities remained unchanged, the sessions provided her with a confidante, someone who genuinely understood and empathised with her journey.

When the school officially inaugurated the young carers support group a few months later, a cocktail of excitement and trepidation surged through Olivia. The intimacy and confidentiality of her sessions with Tania stood in sharp contrast to this new setting, where she'd be sharing her story with fellow students. However, a comforting thought lingered: these were students who, like her, bore the weight of being young carers. Likely, they too harboured their own anxieties and would empathise with Olivia's home situation.

Tania led the inaugural session of the young carers support group, but she soon introduced Mikaela, a seasoned counsellor and art therapist who would be facilitating future sessions. Olivia was joined by four other students: a 16-year-old boy, two girls from year 9 who were a few years older than her, and an eight-year-old girl. The first session was gentle, allowing participants to familiarise themselves with one another. Introductions revolved around basic details like names and ages, without delving into the intimate details of their lives as young carers. Mikaela outlined the roadmap for the sessions, sharing videos and materials that helped define the concept of a 'young carer'. She emphasised the importance of maintaining confidentiality within the group and assured them that they were under no obligation to disclose any information they weren't comfortable with.

As the sessions progressed, bonds began to form. The friendship among the five attendees grew, and strong connections blossomed. Olivia found a close friend in Martha, one of the year 9 girls. They shared a painful commonality: both were caretakers for mothers grappling with mental illnesses.

In Martha's case, her mother was battling bipolar disorder. The two girls began spending time together during school breaks and occasionally on weekends. When Martha's mother suffered a severe episode and had to be hospitalised, Olivia was right there, offering support and a shoulder to lean on. Recognising Martha's distress, Olivia extended an invitation for her to spend the night at her home, an offer Martha gratefully accepted after securing her father's consent. For Olivia, having a friend stay overnight was an unfamiliar experience. She had always hesitated to invite anyone over, fearing judgement or pity regarding her family and her mother's condition. But with Martha, it was different. Olivia sensed Martha would empathise, and she did. Martha not only understood the situation but actively pitched in where she could, helping to tidy the house or take care of Benjamin.

As the days turned into weeks, the bond between Olivia and Martha only deepened. They also grew closer to the other young carers in the group, forging a tight-knit community of support. A few months in, the group welcomed another member – a girl from Olivia's year, though in a different class. The existing members embraced her warmly, ensuring she felt integrated into their circle.

The group sessions, under Mikaela's guidance, were dynamic in nature. On some days, they indulged in artistic activities. Mikaela often began sessions by offering members an opportunity to voice any pressing concerns or feelings. Depending on the group's needs, sessions might focus on supporting a member going through a particularly challenging time, or discussions might revolve around diverse topics, sometimes even unrelated to caregiving. At other times, Mikaela would steer the sessions based on a pre-decided agenda, introducing valuable information or topics to the group. In one of their group sessions, Mikaela introduced the members to a young carers club that had been set up locally by an NGO. This club offered more than just group meetings: it provided a range of support services. Mikaela explained that aside from the regular group sessions, the club offered individual counselling, respite services — which entailed arranging for someone to oversee the care of the relative, granting the young carer a brief respite — and they even organised weekend outings, such as museum visits and other cultural excursions. Mikaela mentioned that if any of the school group members were interested in exploring what the club had to offer, she could make a direct referral. This would allow representatives from the club to establish contact. Seeing potential in the extended resources, both Olivia and Martha expressed interest. After Mikaela passed on their details, they were soon contacted by the club's team lead. Both girls underwent individual assessments. Additionally, a club representative paid a visit to their homes, meeting their families to better gauge the most effective way to support each of them. Olivia and Martha smoothly transitioned into the routines of the young carers club. They couldn't make it to every session due to their post-school responsibilities, but the club was incredibly accommodating. Transportation was arranged, with a staff member driving a van to pick up and later drop off the young carers. In some instances, the club even organised caretakers to stay with the family members in need during club hours. Although they couldn't offer this respite service consistently due to limited resources, it was made available occasionally, especially for carers who found it most challenging to leave their dependents.

Upon joining, Olivia was paired with Ana, a dedicated staff member who became her primary point of contact and support. Through their numerous one-on-one meetings, Ana proposed bringing in a social worker to offer additional assistance at home. Initially, Olivia was hesitant, her long-held fears about social services intervening and potentially fracturing her family looming large. But Ana patiently explained that the social worker's role was purely supportive, whether it involved arranging care for Olivia's mum during her tougher phases, or perhaps even facilitating weekly house cleaning to ease Olivia's chores. Taking some time to think it over, Olivia eventually came around to the idea. The next step involved seeking Jane's consent. Jane, having grown more aware of the strain her condition placed on Olivia especially after Ana's visits, readily agreed. She recognised her limitations and felt guilty about the burden her health placed on her children. Despite sometimes feeling embarrassed about her condition, Jane resolved to be more receptive to external assistance, prioritising her children's well-being. A few weeks later, the family welcomed their first visit from the social worker. While an assessment was required, Ana had already provided a preliminary overview of the family's situation to the social worker, with explicit permission from both Olivia and Jane. Following the assessment, the social worker arranged for regular weekly cleaning assistance. Additionally, she committed to monthly check-ins at Olivia's home, ensuring a consistent touchpoint to gauge the family's well-being and determine if any further support was needed.

Reflecting on her journey, Olivia is amazed at the transformation her life has undergone since that pivotal day she reached out to the young carers lead at school. She vividly recalls the once-overwhelming anxiety, the fear of judgement, and the haunting possibility of her family being torn apart. Yet, in stark contrast, her brave step towards seeking help has only yielded positive outcomes. Not only does she have a robust support system both within and outside the school, but she also benefits from regular home

assistance. The friendships she's forged, particularly with fellow young carers, are profoundly enriching, rooted in mutual understanding. Beyond her immediate circle, there's a domino effect: other students, previously oblivious to the challenges faced by young carers, have become empathetic allies, a clear indicator of the school's successful awareness campaigns about young carers.

Olivia has now found the freedom to share her feelings openly and seek the support she once felt was out of reach. Her mental health has notably improved, with the weight of her burdens lessened. She's discovered a community of young carers, individuals with whom she can connect. Sharing stories of their challenges and the impact of their caregiving roles has been a therapeutic exercise for her. With the extra assistance she's received at home, Olivia's academic performance has improved.

She's now attending after-school study groups, which have made a significant difference. Furthermore, Jane, Olivia's mother, has become more attuned to the sacrifices and pressures Olivia faces as a young carer, striving to ease the burden when she can.

Olivia said that if she could offer any advice to young carers who remain hesitant about seeking support, it would be simple: take the step. She'd emphasise that they aren't alone in their struggles. Even if some areas lack resources or awareness for young carers, confiding in a trusted figure, like a school teacher or social worker, can make all the difference. Olivia's message would be clear: raise your voice, seek the help you deserve. No young carer should feel alone in their journey.

Bibliography

Aldridge, J., & Becker, S. (1993). *Children who care: Inside the world of young carers*. Loughborough, UK: Young Carers Research Group.

Aldridge, J., & Becker, S. (2003). *Children caring for parents with mental illness: Perspectives of young carers, parents and professionals*. The Policy Press.

Armstrong, C. (2002). Behind closed doors: Living with a parent's mental illness. *YoungMinds Magazine*, *61*, 28–30.

Banks, P., Cogan, N., Riddell, S., Deeley, S., Hill, M., & Lisdail, K. (2002). Does the covert nature of caring prohibit the development of effective services for young carers? *British Journal of Guidance & Counselling*, *30*(3), 229–246.

Barber, M., & Siskowski, C. (2008). Youth caregivers: Unrecognised providers of care. *Paediatrics*, *121*(4), 873–874.

Becker, S. (1995). *Young carers in Europe: An exploratory cross-national study in Britain, France, Sweden, and Germany*. Loughborough, Leics: Loughborough Univesity. Young Carers Research Group.

Becker, S. (2000). Young carers. In M. Davies (Ed.), *The Blackwell Encyclopaedia of Social Work* (p. 378). Oxford: Blackwell.

Becker, S. (2008). Informal family carers. In K. Wilson, G. Ruch, M. Lymbery, & A. Cooper (Eds.), *Social work: An introduction to contemporary practice* (pp. 431–460). Pearson Education Limited

Becker, S., & Sempik, J. (2018). Young adult carers: The impact of caring on health and education. *33*(4), 377–386. *Children and Society*. https://doi.org/10.1111/chso.12310

Becker, S. (2019). *Young Carers in Europe*. Loughborough. Young Carers Research Group.

Berardini, Y., Chalmers, H., & Ramey, H. (2021). Unfolding what self-compassion means in young carers' lives. *Child and Adolescent Social Work Journal*, *38*(5), 533–545.

Bolas, H., Wersch, A. V., & Flynn, D. (2007). The well-being of young people who care for a dependent relative: An interpretative phenomenological analysis. *Psychology and Health*, 22(7), 829–850. https://doi.org/10.1080/14768320601020154

Carers Trust. (2022). About young carers. https://carers.org/about-caring/about-young-carers

Crabtree, H., & Warner, L. (1999). *Too much to take on: A report on young carers and bullying*. London: The Princess Royal Trust for Carers.

Cree, V. E. (2003). Worries and problems of young carers: issues for mental health. *Child & Family Social Work*, *8*(4), 301–309.

Dearden, C., Aldridge, J., & Horwath, J. (2010). Young carers: Needs, rights and assessments. In *The child's world: The comprehensive guide to assessing children in need* (pp. 214–228).

Dearden, C., & Becker, S. (1998). *Young carers in the United Kingdom: A profile*. London: Carers National Association.

Dearden, C., & Becker, S. (2000). *Growing up caring: Vulnerability and transition to adulthood – Young carers' experiences*. York: Youth Work Press for the Joseph Rowntree Foundation.

Dearden, C., & Becker, S. (2004). *Young carers in the UK: The 2004 report*. London:Carers UK.

Dharampal, R., & Ani, C. (2020). The emotional and mental health needs of young carers: What psychiatry can do. *BJPsych Bulletin*, *44*(3), 112–120.

Dunn, B. (1993). Growing up with a psychotic mother: A retrospective study. *American Journal of Orthopsychiatry*, *63*, 177–189.

Earley, L., & Cushway, D. (2002). The parentified child. *Clinical Child Psychology and Psychiatry*, 7(2), 163–178. https://doi.org/10.1177/1359104502007002005

Family Action. (2012). BE BOTHERED! Making education count for young carers. https://www.family-action.org.uk/content/

uploads/2014/06/Be-Bothered-Make-Education-Count-for-Young-Carers.pdf.

Frank, J. (1995). *Couldn't care more: A study of young carers and their needs*. The Children's Society.

Frank, J., Tatum, C., & Tucker, S. (1999). *On small shoulders: Learning from the experiences of former young carers*. London: The Children's Society UK.

Frank, J., & McLarnon, J. (2008). *Young carers, parents and their families: Key principles of practice. Supportive practice guidance for those who work directly with, or commission services for, young carers and their families*. The Children's Society.

Hill, S. (1999). The physical effects of caring on children. *Journal of Young Carers Work*, 3, 6–7.

Joseph, S., Becker, F., Becker, S., & Regel, S. (2009). Manual for measures of caring activities and outcomes for children and young people. Carers Trust. https://carers.org/resources/all-resources/101-manual-for-measures-of-caring-activities-and-outcomes-for-children-and-young-people

Marsden, R. (1995). *Young carers and education*. Borough of Enfield, Education Department.

McClure, L. (2001). School-age caregivers: Perceptions of school nurses working in central England. *The Journal of School Nursing*, *17*(2), 76–82.

McCormack, L., White, S., & Cuenca, J. (2017). A fractured journey of growth: Making meaning of a 'broken' childhood and parental mental ill-health. *Community, Work & Family*, *20*(3), 327–345. http://dx.doi.org/10.1080/13668803.2015.1117418

Mortimore, P. (1995). The positive effects of schooling. In M. Rutter (Ed.), *Psychosocial disturbances in young people: Challenge for prevention* (pp. 333–366). Cambridge: Cambridge University Press.

Noble-Carr, D. (2002). *Young carers research project: Background papers*. Canberra: Carers Australia.

Roling, M., Falkson, S., Hellmers, C., & Metzing, S. (2020). Early caregiving experiences and the impact on transition into adulthood and further life: A literature review. *Scandinavian Journal of Caring Sciences*, *34*(3), 539–551.

Szafran, O., Torti, J., Waugh, E., & Duerksen, K. (2016). Former young carers reflect on their caregiving experience. *Canadian Journal of Family and Youth*, *8*(1), 129–151. http://ejournals.library.ualberta.ca/index/php/cjfy

Thomas, N., Stainton, T., Jackson, S., Cheung, W. Y., Doubtfire, S., & Webb, A. (2003). Your friends don't understand: Invisibility and unmet need in the lives of 'young carers'. *Child & Family Social Work*, *8*(1), 35–46.

Wepf, H., Joseph, S., & Leu, A. (2022). Benefit finding moderates the relationship between young carer experiences and mental well-being. *Psychology & health*, *37*(10), 1270–1286.

Yeandle, S., Bennett, C., Buckner, L., Fry, G., & Price, C. (2007). Carers, employment and services in Leeds. *CES Report Series*, 10.